PUBLICATIONS OF THE

## MINNESOTA HISTORICAL SOCIETY

Russell W. Fridley, *Director*

June Drenning Holmquist, *Assistant Director for Publications and Research*

MINNESOTA HISTORIC SITES
PAMPHLET SERIES No. 4

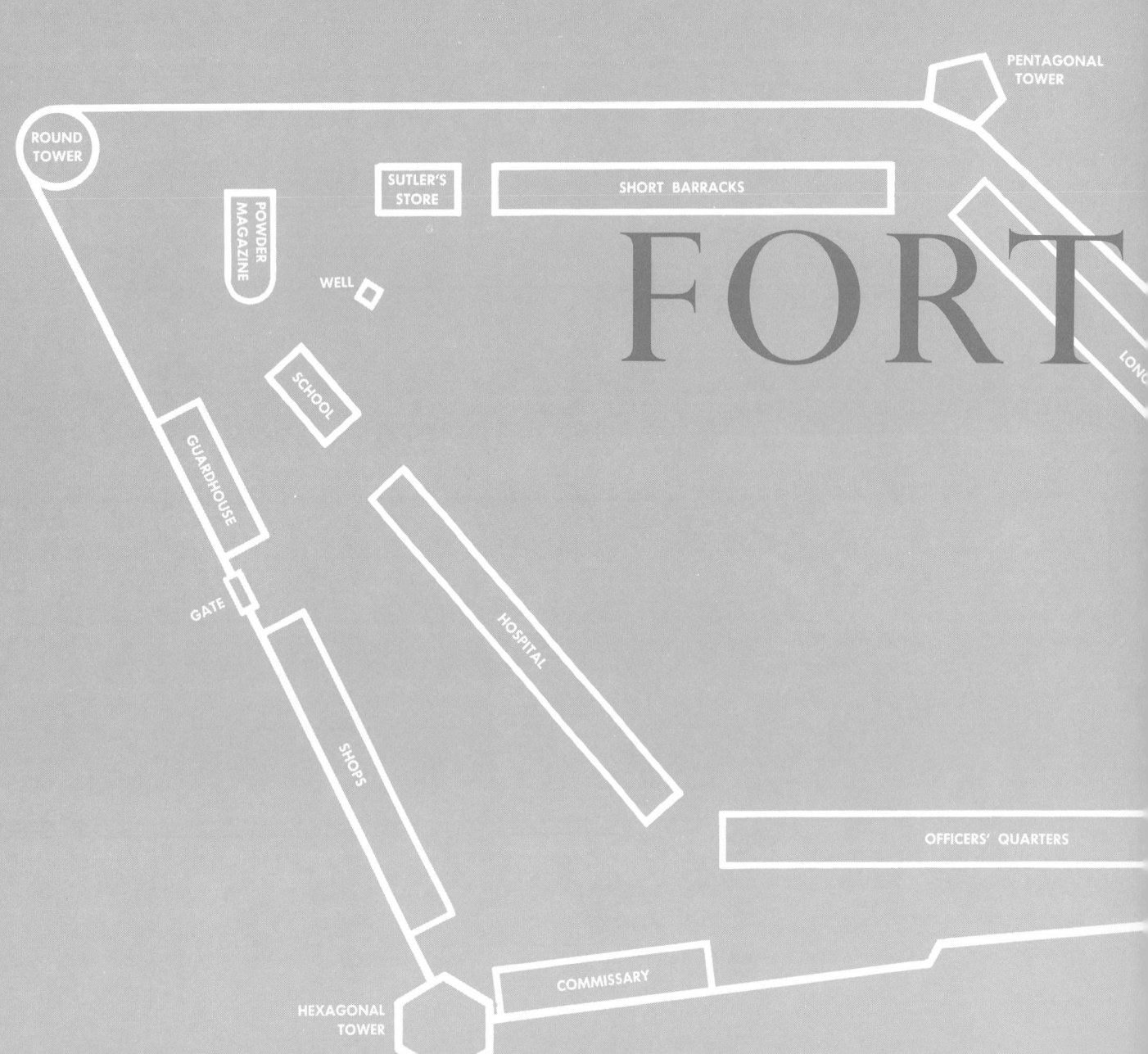

# SNELLING

*Anchor Post of the Northwest*

By Marilyn Ziebarth and Alan Ominsky

MINNESOTA HISTORICAL SOCIETY • 1970

Copyright 1970 © by the
MINNESOTA HISTORICAL SOCIETY

*Second printing, 1979*

NO PORTION OF THIS BOOKLET MAY BE REPRODUCED IN ANY FORM WITHOUT THE WRITTEN PERMISSION OF THE MINNESOTA HISTORICAL SOCIETY.

*Library of Congress Card Catalog Number: 70-121443*
*Standard Book Number: 87351-061-5*

*The Minnesota Historical Society wishes to express its appreciation to the Fort Snelling Sesquicentennial Committee for financial aid that helped to make this publication possible.*

In 1820 when Josiah Snelling laid the cornerstone, the fortress that became Fort Snelling was the only United States military post in the Northwest north of a line from Prairie du Chien, Wisconsin, to the Pacific. Scenically and strategically located on the crest of the bluff above the junction of the Minnesota and Mississippi rivers, the fort was the only tangible evidence of United States sovereignty in a vast unsettled wilderness, keeping an uneasy peace between the Sioux and Chippewa Indians.

Within its walls, the first school in Minnesota opened its doors in 1823, and the first hospital and circulating library came into being. The fort's brass band and its amateur theater were the first such entertainments on the Minnesota frontier, and the first Protestant church in the area was organized there. The post's commandant directed the first development of the region's natural resources, harnessing the water power of the Falls of St. Anthony to run Minnesota's first sawmill and gristmill. Near its walls gathered the pioneers who founded the Twin Cities of St. Paul and Minneapolis.

Fort Snelling was the region's first military post and the cradle of settlement in the Northwest. It played these roles alone for thirty years until Minnesota entered the Union as a territory in 1849. In the 1860s it served as a rendezvous point for all the Minnesota troops mustered into the Union Army during the Civil War, and its military functions continued through all of the nation's wars until 1946, when the old fort's 126-year career as an army post came to an end.

In the 1950s Fort Snelling began a new career as archaeologists searched for clues to its long-disappeared structures. Beginning in the 1960s, with funds supplied by the Minnesota legislature, it rose again — reconstructed in authentic detail as it looked when the Sioux and Chippewa gathered in its shadow, when explorers and traders sought it as an oasis of civilization, and when pioneers took up the first land legally open for settlement in Minnesota.

By 1970 — the 150th anniversary of the laying of its cornerstone — the old fort served as an oasis of a different kind, a green historic site, surrounded by free-

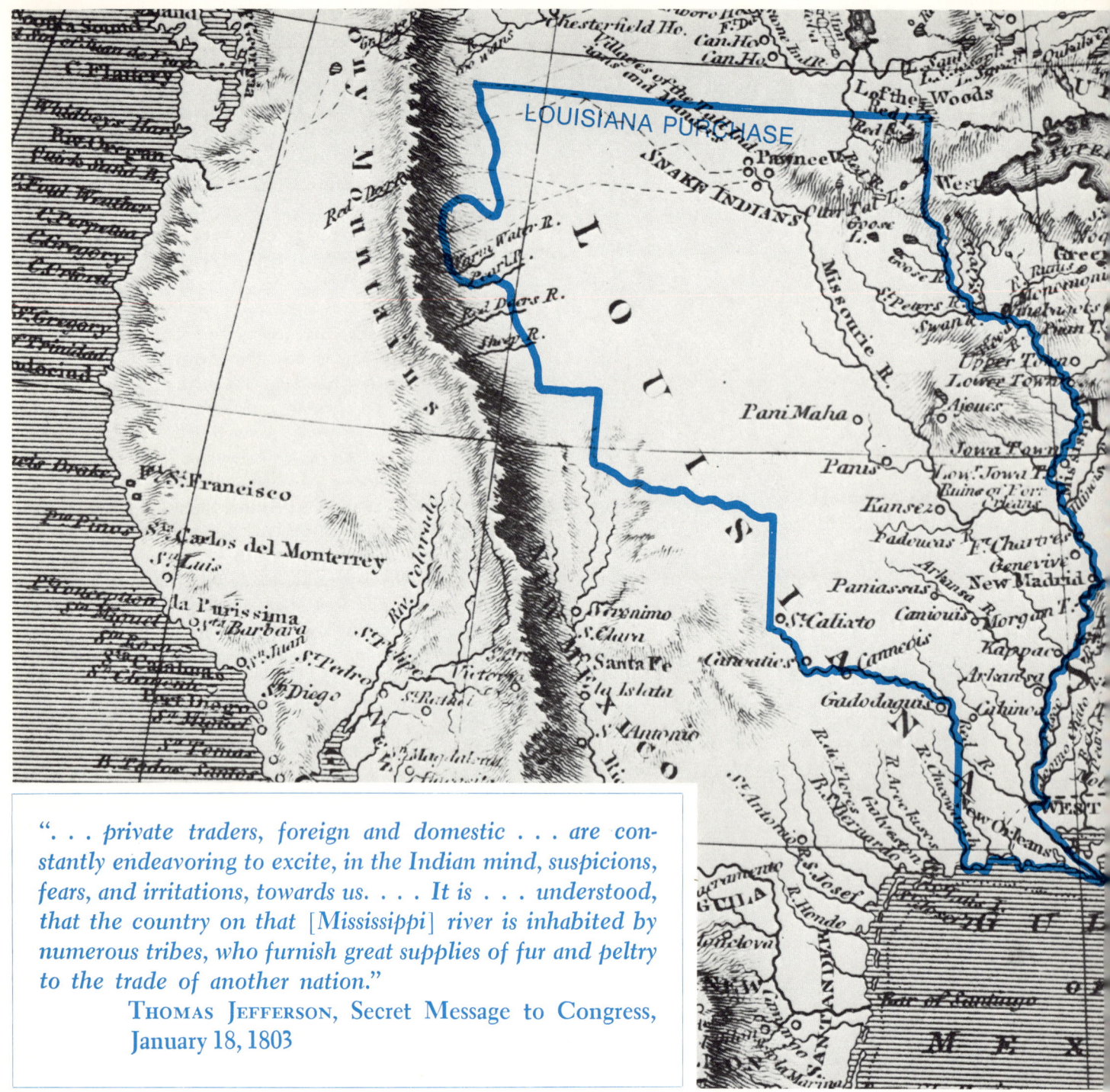

"... private traders, foreign and domestic ... are constantly endeavoring to excite, in the Indian mind, suspicions, fears, and irritations, towards us. ... It is ... understood, that the country on that [Mississippi] river is inhabited by numerous tribes, who furnish great supplies of fur and peltry to the trade of another nation."

    THOMAS JEFFERSON, Secret Message to Congress, January 18, 1803

THE LOUISIANA PURCHASE (1803) expanded the United States westward across the Mississippi River to the Rocky Mountains. During the next few years the government moved to explore the vast new territory and attempted unsuccessfully to control the fur trade and reduce British influence among the Indians. Base map from Rees' *Cyclopædia* [1806?]

ways and jet aircraft, where visitors of all ages could glimpse a rich heritage and see a living reminder of a simpler age when the foundations of modern commonwealths were laid by men protected by the rough-hewn walls of this frontier outpost.

If the United States had not built such a garrison, the history of the northwestern states might have been radically different, for European colonial powers had owned or coveted the land drained by the Mississippi River's western tributaries for centuries. France took the area from war-weakened Spain in the late 18th century, and British fur traders exploited the region's natural wealth through an extensive system of fur trading posts. Fearing that the increasingly populous United States (only ten persons per inhabited square mile in 1786!) might come into conflict with these nations over the western territory, American politicians such as Thomas Jefferson urged that the land be annexed.

When he became president in 1801, Jefferson acted decisively to secure this region. Although the federal Constitution did not explicitly authorize the acquisition of new areas, he purchased the vaguely defined Louisiana Territory from France in 1803. For a meager $15 million the United States obtained some 800,000 square miles of rich land (including most of present-day Minnesota) between the Mississippi River and the Rocky Mountains.

British fur traders ignored the transfer of sovereignty, and Jefferson realized that only knowledge and physical occupation of the area would ensure American authority. In 1804 he sent Meriwether Lewis and William Clark to explore the upper reaches of the Missouri River. A year later Zebulon M. Pike (for whom Pikes Peak was later named) was sent to investigate the Upper Mississippi River and to "select and purchase suitable sites for the building of permanent fortifications."

On September 21, 1805, Pike camped at the junction of the St. Peter's (now the Minnesota) and Mississippi rivers. For $200 worth of rum and presents he concluded an agreement with the resident Sioux Indians for an area including most of present-day Minneapolis and St. Paul, promising to pay them $2,000.

3

WHILE LEWIS AND CLARK were exploring the western reaches of the Louisiana Purchase, Lieut. Zebulon M. Pike was dispatched to the Upper Mississippi in 1805 to treat with the Indians and select sites for future military posts. Courtesy National Archives, Washington, D.C.

*"On the lakes, the Mississippi, Missouri, Arkansas, and Red River, our posts are now, or will be shortly, extended, for the protection of our trade and the preservation of the peace of the frontiers, to Green Bay, the mouths of the St. Peter's and the Yellow Stone river, Bellepoint, and Natchitoches."*

JOHN C. CALHOUN to House of Representatives, December 14, 1818

*". . . the Chief's entered. I addressed them in a Speech which though long, and touching on many points, yet the principal ones were the Granting of the Land . . . and the making peace with the Chippeway's. . . . They gave me the Land required . . . but spoke doubtfully relative to the peace."*

ZEBULON M. PIKE journal, September 23, 1805

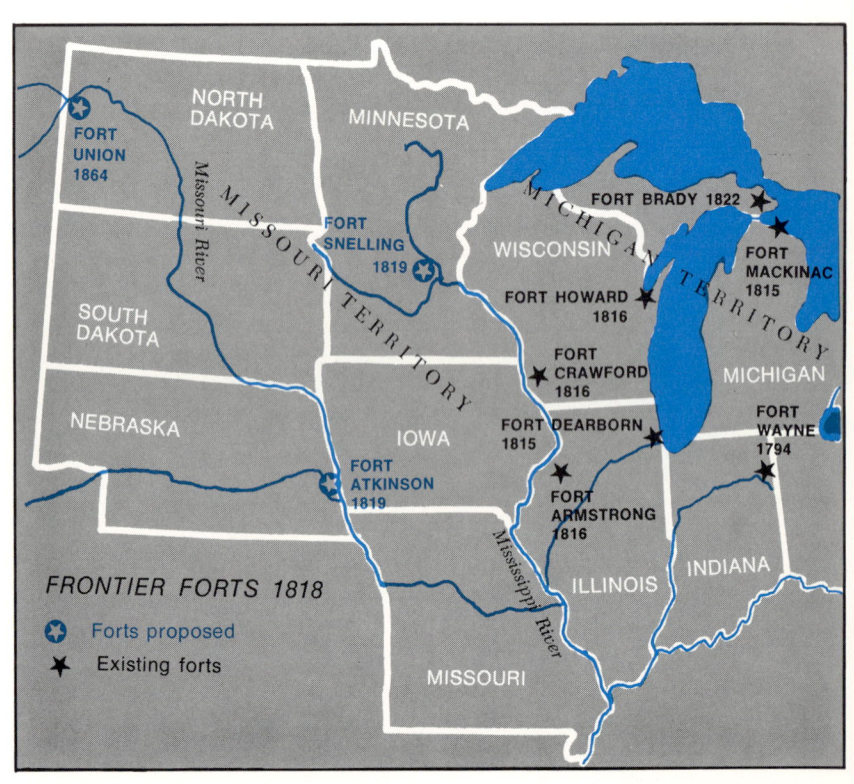

4

FOLLOWING the War of 1812, John C. Calhoun, secretary of war in President James Monroe's cabinet, suggested a plan for the defense of the western frontier which led to the construction of Fort Snelling fifteen years after Pike's visit.

IN 1817 Major Stephen H. Long ascended the Mississippi in a six-oared skiff. He confirmed Pike's selection at the junction of the Minnesota River and recommended the actual site where Fort Snelling was later built. Courtesy Independence Hall Collection, Philadelphia.

The government did not move immediately to build a military post on the land Pike selected, and British influence in the Northwest remained unchecked when the United States declared war on England in 1812. British partisans on the frontier organized the Indians to raid American settlements, including that at Prairie du Chien, Wisconsin, and although the war ended in victory for the United States, the British seemed firmly in control of the valuable fur trade of the region.

Realizing that action was necessary to establish American authority over the sprawling area Jefferson had purchased, John C. Calhoun, secretary of war in James Monroe's cabinet from 1817 to 1825, proposed the establishment of an ambitious system of forts. Calhoun's strategy called for a chain of posts stretching from Detroit southward to St. Louis and westward to the Upper Missouri. In the west he planned to locate posts on the Yellowstone and Missouri rivers and to erect a major fortification at the Minnesota River junction "purchased" earlier by Pike. A comprehensive system of forts and interconnecting trails, Calhoun believed, would secure the frontier from British infiltration, and "the most valuable fur trade in the world would be thrown into our hands." The Minnesota post, he cautioned, should be exceptionally strong because of its "proximity" to the powerful Sioux and to the British Red River Colony near present-day Winnipeg.

In 1817 Calhoun commissioned Major Stephen H. Long, a topographical engineer, to inspect Pike's site for the key northernmost fort. Long confirmed Pike's choice, and on February 10, 1819, the secretary of war ordered the Fifth Regiment of Infantry to move westward from Detroit for the purpose of constructing a fort. Lieut. Colonel Henry Leavenworth was chosen to command the expedition.

The rest of the plan envisioned by Calhoun was not carried out. Only the Minnesota post and Fort Atkinson in Nebraska were initiated in 1819. The proposed Yellowstone fort and the interconnecting system of roads and waterways did not materialize, as Congress, disgruntled with the management of the undertaking, refused to grant further funds. Consequently the anchor fort at the mouth of the Minnesota assumed added importance in the defense of the frontier. Stand-

**LIEUT. COLONEL HENRY LEAVENWORTH** commanded the troops of the Fifth Infantry sent to erect the new northern post in 1819. Before much was done, he was replaced by Col. Josiah Snelling in a way that infuriated him.

**COLONEL SNELLING** designed the stone fort later named for him. On September 10, 1820, he laid the cornerstone. By 1824 he was able to report that the buildings had been completed.

> "I am happy to have you take command of your Regiment, but candour requires me to say, that I feel injured by the manner in which you have done it."
> LEAVENWORTH to SNELLING,
> August 13, 1820

> ". . . Col. Wool neither directly or indirectly, said any thing which implied disapprobation of your Conduct while in command at St. Peters, indeed, the reverse was the case, for he left me under the conviction that his report of the 5th Regt. and its commander would be in the highest degree favourable."
> SNELLING to LEAVENWORTH,
> August 20, 1820

> "The Colonel's hair was quite red. He was also slightly bald. From this peculiarity the soldiers nick-named him, among themselves, the 'prairie-hen.' . . .
>
> "Intemperance, among both officers and men . . . was an almost universal thing, and produced deplorable effects. I regret to say that the commandant was no exception to this rule. Usually kind and pleasant, when one of his convivial spells occurred, he would act furious, sometimes getting up in the night and making a scene. He was severe in his treatment of the men who committed a like indiscretion."
>
> **Reminiscences of ANN ADAMS, a refugee from the Red River Colony**

THIS VIEW of the interior of the fort shows it very much as it looked when Snelling completed his work in 1824. *Harper's New Monthly Magazine*, July, 1853.

ing alone for nearly thirty years — between Fort Crawford 200 miles to the south, the British border to the north, and the Pacific to the west — Fort Snelling's influence extended over a wide area, which included the Missouri River country.

Although his orders had been written in February, Lieut. Colonel Henry Leavenworth did not reach the Minnesota River until August 24, 1819, dangerously late in the northern season. With him were "ninety-eight rank and file" soldiers, twenty special men to maneuver the unwieldy supply boats, and Indian Agent Thomas Forsyth, who had been hurriedly dispatched from St. Louis to deal with the Sioux.

Forsyth and Leavenworth conveyed their intention of building a fort to the local Sioux chiefs (including Red Wing, Little Crow, and Wabasha). They warned the Indians of the folly of resisting this effort and emphasized the benefits of the outpost to the Indians in the form of a blacksmith shop and a trading post. Then Forsyth distributed $2,000 worth of goods and trinkets — the payment which Pike had promised fourteen years earlier.

Leavenworth elected to build a temporary camp in a low, mosquito-infested spot near the southeast end of the present Mendota Bridge. Despite the arrival of 120 additional soldiers in September, progress was slow, and the party — including three officers' wives and one newborn baby — lived on the boats for weeks before crude log huts and a stockade were completed. With unintended irony, the camp was named "Cantonment New Hope."

The winter of 1819–20 at New Hope taught the group some lessons in frontier survival. The hastily erected huts gave little protection against below zero temperatures. Meals unvaryingly consisted of tainted meat and moldy bread augmented by small amounts of game and vegetables purchased from the Indians. Many soldiers fell victim to scurvy; scarcely enough healthy men were left to care for the sick and bury the dead. Although the disease was finally controlled "by administering spruce tea and other vegetable decoctions," Leavenworth moved with the arrival of warmer weather and

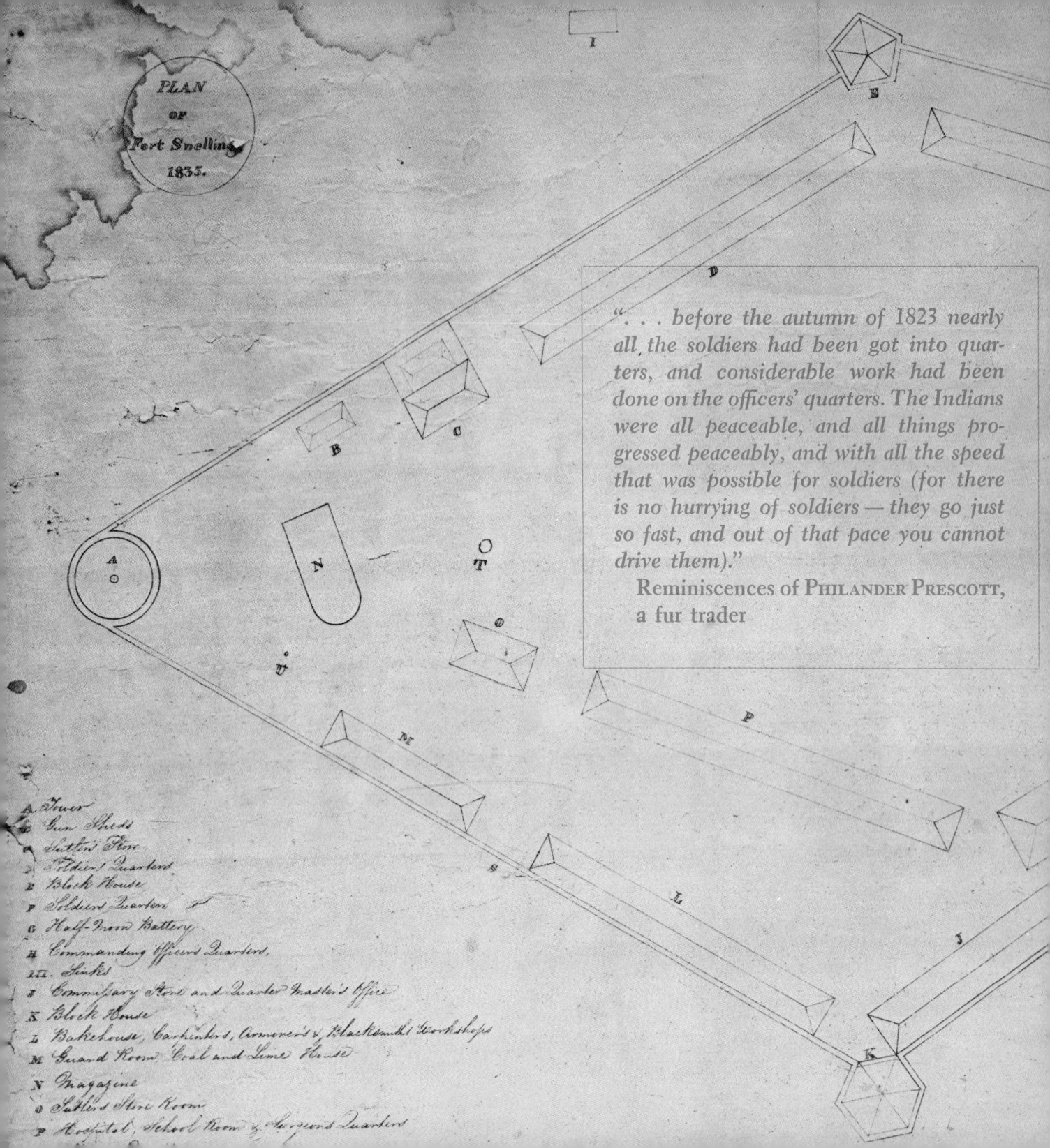

"... before the autumn of 1823 nearly all the soldiers had been got into quarters, and considerable work had been done on the officers' quarters. The Indians were all peaceable, and all things progressed peaceably, and with all the speed that was possible for soldiers (for there is no hurrying of soldiers — they go just so fast, and out of that pace you cannot drive them)."

Reminiscences of PHILANDER PRESCOTT, a fur trader

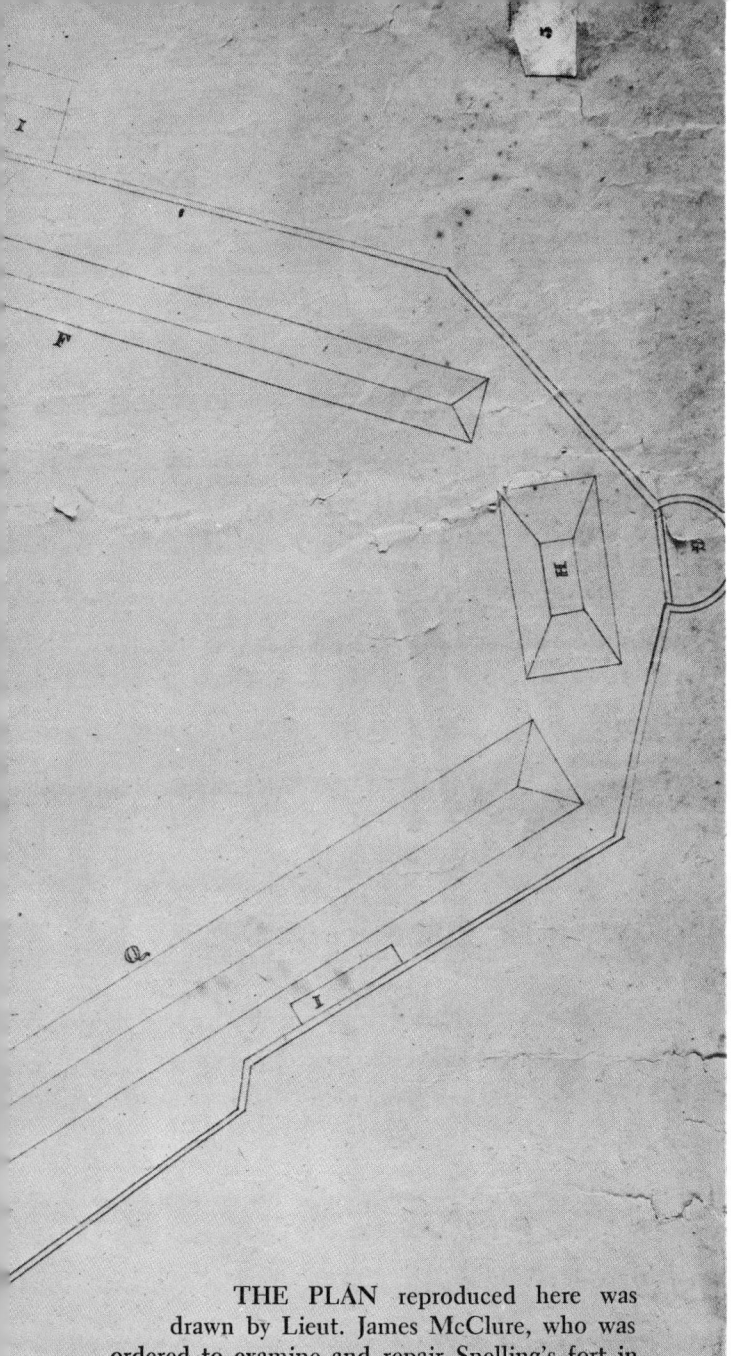

THE PLAN reproduced here was drawn by Lieut. James McClure, who was ordered to examine and repair Snelling's fort in 1835. It is the earliest known scale drawing of the completed post, and it served as the starting point for research on the restoration of old Fort Snelling in the 1960s. Courtesy National Archives.

spring floods from the river flat to tents pitched on a high bluff above the Mississippi River (near the present Bureau of Mines building). Named for the nearby (and still flowing) spring, the new site was called "Camp Coldwater."

Turning his attention to a permanent fortification, Leavenworth decided to build a square log fort on a rise of ground northwest of the eventual site of Fort Snelling. Although his men began cutting logs and floating them to this spot, Leavenworth had accomplished very little by the summer of 1820, when he was abruptly relieved of his assignment by Colonel Josiah Snelling.

Snelling formally assumed command in June, 1820, two months before reaching the site, and the timing and manner of his appointment were unusual. Possibly Leavenworth's superiors felt that he did not exhibit the initiative needed to plan and construct a wilderness fort. This may be inferred from a letter in which Leavenworth requested specific instructions about the kind of fort he should build and from his hesitation to begin work without official authorization — although it was not until 1834 that construction plans for military buildings were prepared and approved in Washington.

Snelling's breach of etiquette in assuming command before he appeared on the scene provoked Leavenworth's lasting hostility. The men continued their quarrel in a St. Louis newspaper until 1823 when Leavenworth refused to broach the subject again.

Red-haired Josiah Snelling proved to be an excellent choice for commandant of the yet-to-be-built fort. Thirty-eight years old in 1820 and a veteran officer who had served in the War of 1812, he was capable and courageous, but "impetuous" and "irascible" when in his cups. Possessing the confidence and resourcefulness required for his wilderness task, Snelling "infused system and energy among men and officers." A harsh disciplinarian who occasionally administered legal punishments with the cat-o'-nine-tails, he took no pleasure in meaningless drills and formal parades. On September 10, 1820, one month after his arrival, Snelling laid the cornerstone for a fort downriver from Leavenworth's site on the high promontory which Major Long had recommended.

*"We are here entirely out of the world, & very seldom hear from the civilized part of our country, as we have no regular mailes; it was the 26 of May this year, when the first Steam Boat reached here. . . . Although this is unquestionably the most exposed post in the nation, & fartherest from supporting distance, there are only three comp$^s$ assigned to it, which are reduced to less than 100 men, & I calculate before we receive a re-enforcement I shall not have men enough to mount a guard sufficiently strong to post the centinels at hailing distance around this extensive work."*

**ZACHARY TAYLOR to DR. THOMAS LAWSON, August 28, 1828**

LIBRARIES far and near were combed for information, and some interesting discoveries were made when the records were assembled at the Minnesota Historical Society. For example, sentry boxes were mentioned in early letters, but it was not known what they looked like. When the pencil sketch of a sentry box by Capt. Seth Eastman was found in the Peabody Museum at Harvard University and the plan, drawn in 1839, turned up in the National Archives, it became possible to locate and reconstruct the sentinel posts. The circled areas in the plan showed where the guards were stationed.

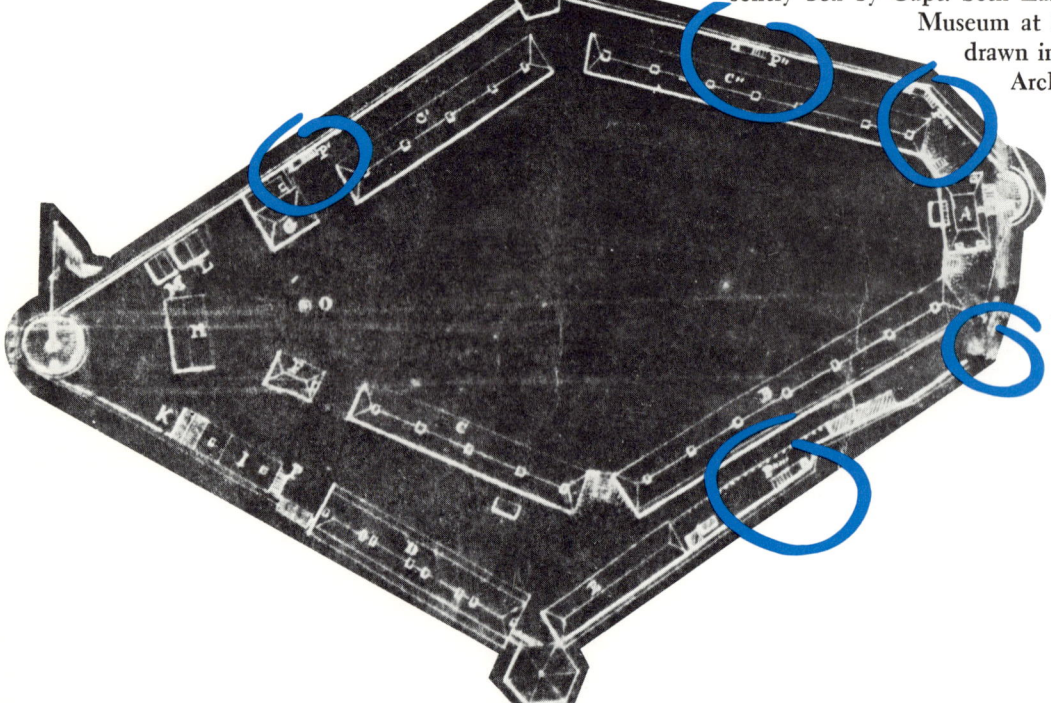

MANY DOCUMENTS were collected to depict life at Fort Snelling. These records kept by the post surgeon showed that a cold snap occurred on January 5, 1823, when the temperature dipped to 28 below zero. Such weather notes were kept at the post, then called Fort St. Anthony, from the time the troops arrived in 1819. They were found in the National Archives.

The colonel not only rejected Leavenworth's site; he also elected to build the post primarily of stone rather than wood, choosing an irregular diamond shape "to adapt it to the shape of the ground on which it stands." Without the customary military engineer and lacking a skilled civilian construction crew, Snelling relied heavily on the talents of Lieut. Robert A. McCabe, who acted as his engineer and received a promotion for his work. Together the two men drew up plans which utilized the building materials in the area and the labor of the soldiers, who were paid about $6 a month plus 15¢ extra per day for their work.

Throughout the winter of 1820–21, Snelling's men cut logs on the Rum River north of the fort site so that the timber could be floated down when the ice went out the following spring. To make lumber for furniture and outbuildings, the soldiers completed in 1822 the first sawmill erected in Minnesota, harnessing the water power of the Falls of St. Anthony to run it. (A gristmill was also built at the Falls in 1824 to grind grain grown at the fort in the extensive gardens planted at Snelling's insistence to augment the soldiers' meager food supplies.)

The colonel also set his men to work quarrying the native limestone along the river bluffs. The fortress he planned was to have four corner towers linked by an interconnecting stone wall. One tower was to be semicircular, one pentagonal, one round, and one hexagonal, and they were to be constructed to assure the best angle of fire against would-be attackers. Snelling would have preferred to build the entire fort of stone, but there were more carpenters than masons among his troops. As a result, he ordered that the long barracks and officers' quarters be constructed of wood.

Under Snelling's able direction the post, which was first called Fort St. Anthony, quickly took shape. By the summer of 1823, three barracks (two of stone and one of wood) were in use, and the officers' quarters, walls, and four towers were nearly finished. One of the stone barracks served as the hospital. Describing the completed fort in 1824, Snelling reported that, in addition to these buildings, there were spacious commandant's headquarters; a "Commissaries and Quarter Master's store . . . capable of containing four years

THIS is one of the earliest known photographs of the fort. It is a daguerreotype perhaps taken by Alexander Hesler in the 1850s. Since it shows the Hexagonal Tower and the four-story commissary building, it proved invaluable to the restoration, making it possible to check the accuracy of some of the earlier paintings and drawings by various artists.

THE QUARTERLY REPORTS of the post surgeon, Dr. Nathan S. Jarvis, indicate that respiratory infections like flu and colds ("catarrhus") were a problem in the spring of 1834. Such reports, running through the years, are preserved in the National Archives.

> *". . . we have all have been most of the month shut up in the fort and confin'd to our Rooms owing to the excessive cold. . . . Major Bliss appointed me the other day Librarian & Inspector of the Post school. . . . Our Library contains about 400 vols of excellent books to which is attach'd a Reading Room which is abundantly supply'd with Newspapers & Periodicals. The school has about 20 children belonging in and out of the Fort. . . . My horse took it into his head to die the other day . . . I had him drawn under the walls of the Fort . . . as wolf bait. . . . I have got some pretty Indian curiosities . . . all I want now is a wife, can you pick me out one."*
>
> DR. NATHAN S. JARVIS to his sister MARY, February 2, 1834

THE SECOND HOSPITAL at the fort may be seen over the wall near the gatehouse in this water color painted by Alfred Sully in 1855. Constructed in 1840 by adding a second story to the former shop building, it represented the first major structural change in Snelling's work. Courtesy Thomas Gilcrease Institute of American History and Art, Tulsa.

supply of provisions" (later put to other uses because of its exceeding dampness); a stone workshop building accommodating "Blacksmiths, Carpenters, Wheelrights etc and a Bake house"; a schoolhouse which later served as a chapel and billiard room; a guardhouse with "two cells for solitary confinement"; a vaulted, double-roofed powder magazine with walls 6 feet thick; a sutler's store (similar to today's PX); an "uncommonly cold and clear" well 24 feet deep; and a broad roadway from the river bottom "constructed with immense labor."

Together the buildings formed an imposing, seemingly impregnable fortress symbolizing the authority of the United States. Snelling had built well. The fort's dramatic location and design successfully discouraged any would-be assailants. No attack was ever made upon Fort Snelling in its long years of service on the frontier!

In 1824 General Winfield Scott, conducting the first official inspection of the new post, recommended that it be renamed in honor of its resourceful commander. Early in 1825 the northwesternmost military outpost in the United States officially became Fort Snelling. Its builder remained in charge until 1827 — the first of a long line of distinguished commandants that included Zachary Taylor (1828–29) who later became president of the United States.

Life at the post, as at many other military garrisons, was often a struggle against discomfort and boredom. Records indicate that food, clothing, and shelter were of prime concern to the men — particularly during the long, bleak winters of the early years. Food was limited and lacking in variety. Grasshoppers, blackbirds, and crows regularly and perversely stripped the fort fields, thwarting Snelling's attempts to grow grain.

The supply problems were formidable, for there were no roads, and the river — the life line to the outside world — was frozen half the year. During the particularly severe winter of 1830–31, the fort received no mail for five months. Shipments, often a season late, invariably contained "a surplus of uniform coats, cockades and eagles" and a paucity of work clothing. Sol-

GEORGE CATLIN, a noted artist who was especially interested in the American Indian, was one of many notables to visit the fort. On July 9, 1835, Taliaferro recorded that Catlin observed forty-five Chippewa braves dancing near the agency. The painting (right) is a portion of his rendering of such a dance. Courtesy Smithsonian Institution, Washington, D.C.

UNDER THE GUNS of the fort was the American Fur Company's headquarters across the river at Mendota (below). From there, Henry H. Sibley directed the firm's regional operations and traded with the Indians. Both the Sibley and Faribault houses, which are preserved in Mendota, may be seen in the painting. It is thought to be the work of Sergeant Edward K. Thomas, who was stationed at Fort Snelling in the 1850s. Courtesy Gilcrease Institute.

LAWRENCE TALIAFERRO, Indian agent at the fort during its early years, was painted by an unknown artist, possibly George Catlin. An honest and dedicated man, Taliaferro was an important figure in the history of the area.

*". . . this evening . . . a few minutes after tattoo had finished beating — I heard the report of seven guns. It was soon ascertained to be 9 Sioux who had fired on one of the Chippeway Lodges & wounded 8 of them 3 suffered mortal. . . . They were all brought up immediately to the Council House — and such a scene I have not witnessed before or to the same extent. . . . I sent word early to the Sioux that for this wanton evilly & cowardly conduct they should give satisfaction to the Chippeway — Accordingly one of the murderers was given up & through measures adopted by Colonel Snelling 7 others were taken."*

LAWRENCE TALIAFERRO journal, May 28, 29, 1827

diers augmented their winter wardrobes with blankets, stockings, and moccasins purchased at the sutler's store, but on cold nights they were forced to sleep three in a bed to keep warm.

Whereas most posts hired civilians to supply fuel, the soldiers at Fort Snelling had to collect and haul their own. By 1840 the supply near the post was exhausted, and the estimated 2,000 cords of wood consumed each winter had to be cut ten miles away. A shocked military inspector reported to the secretary of war that "enlisted men in the Northern frontier are now little more than *laborers*. Nearly half of their time is occupied in providing fuel."

Attempts by West Point-trained, city-bred officers to bring "spit and polish" to the frontier fort proved both unsuccessful and unfortunate. According to military inspection records, discipline was usually "Correct — if Discipline mean the enforcement of Subordination *merely*." But when exercises and routines were reported to be "not very perfect," a temporary post commander who considered "drill and discipline . . . paramount to all other objects" suspended summer wood-gathering in order to improve the garrison's drill performance, grievously adding to the harshness of the winter of 1825–26.

Boredom was as big a challenge to the soldiers as the cold weather or the work. In 1826 the 400 books and periodicals of the fort's library — the first in Minnesota — were in such demand that overdue fines ran 12½¢ per day. To entertain themselves the men also created the area's first theater, performing weekly plays by the 1830s in which they took both the male and female parts. Harry Watkins, a fifer who later became famous as a dramatic actor, got his start in such fort productions as *The Lady of Lyons;* he was often chosen for the role of leading lady because of his youth (15 years) and his size (he could wear the commandant's daughter's clothing). Officers' dances and teas were popular, and hoedowns were attended by enlisted men and laundresses, of whom one admirer wrote wryly, "if they do not dance with grace . . . at least make it up in strength and duration, generally continuing it from 8 o'clock in the evening until 8 in the morning."

After 1823 Fort Snelling was not totally isolated. That year the arrival of the "Virginia," carrying tools,

THE Fort Snelling military reservation was carefully mapped in 1839. Squatters living on it were then ordered to move by Major Joseph Plympton. As the map at right indicates, the reservation covered a sizable portion of the present-day Twin Cities. The arrows show the locations of the mills and the chapel pictured below. Courtesy National Archives.

SOME settlers took up land near the mills erected by the soldiers at the Falls of St. Anthony, foreshadowing the later development of Minneapolis. Photograph by B. F. Upton, 1857.

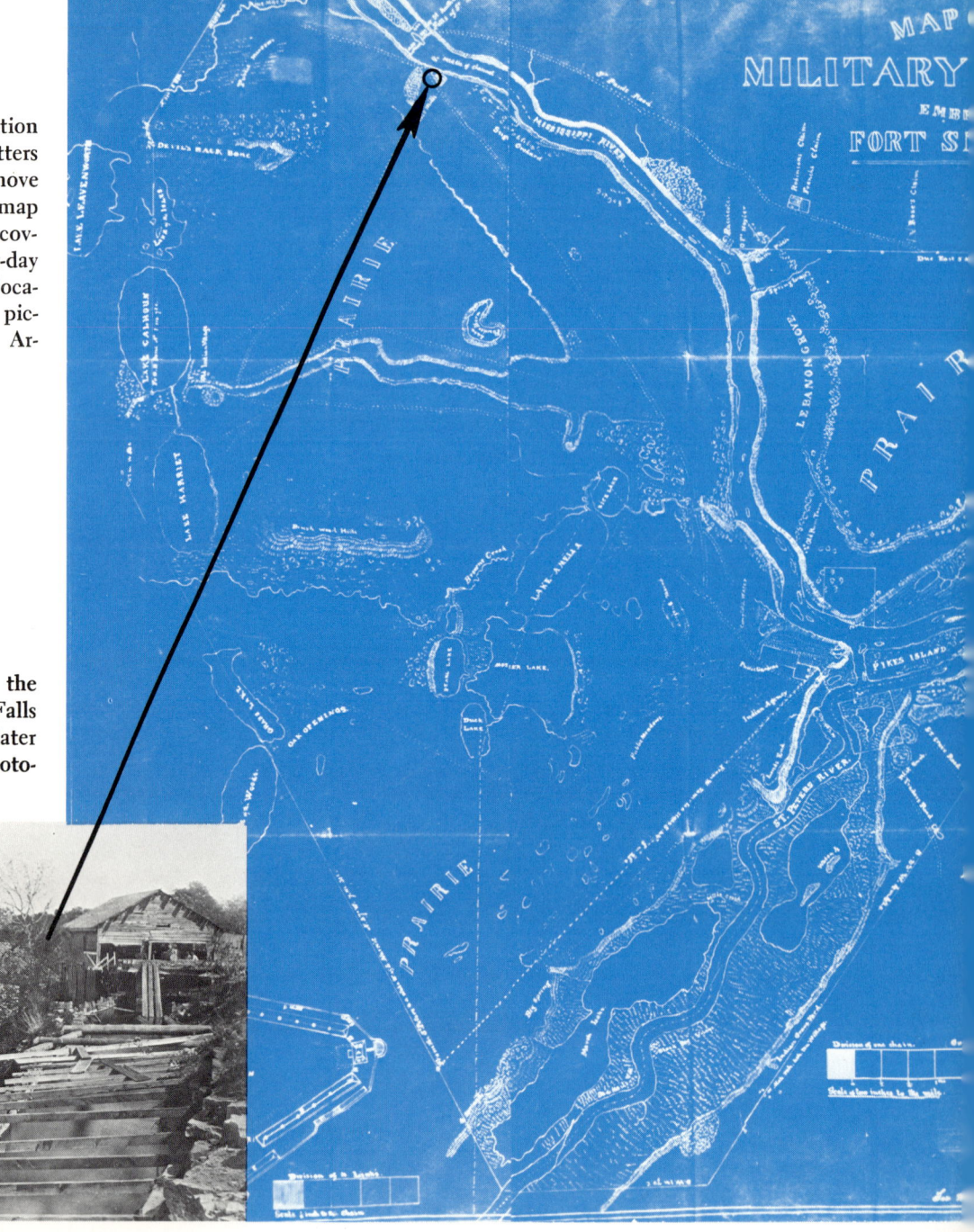

16

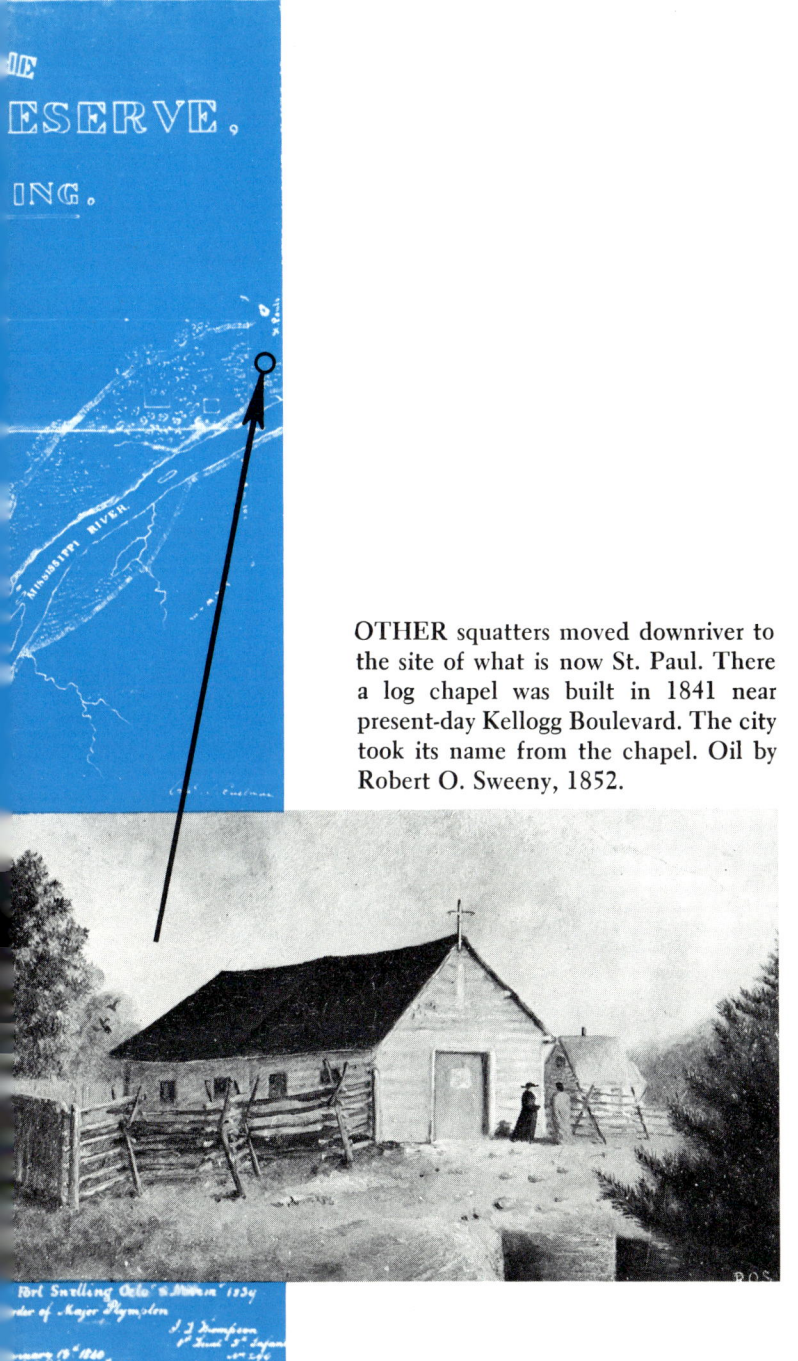

OTHER squatters moved downriver to the site of what is now St. Paul. There a log chapel was built in 1841 near present-day Kellogg Boulevard. The city took its name from the chapel. Oil by Robert O. Sweeny, 1852.

medicines, winter clothing, and mail, marked the beginnings of steamboat service on the Upper Mississippi River. For many years, however, the whistle of a steamboat heralded a festive occasion, and as late as 1833 a soldier observed: "There's generally but 2 steamboats arrive here in a year and they consequently excite considerable stir in this retir'd and insolated spot."

Planted well out beyond the line of white settlement, Fort Snelling at first shared the Upper Mississippi Valley with thousands of Sioux and Chippewa Indians. As planned by Calhoun, its functions were to keep peace between the tribes, destroy British influence, and secure fur trading profits for the United States. Although it successfully achieved two of these goals, the post was never entirely effective in controlling skirmishes between the Sioux and Chippewa.

Initially the army tried to stay out of these conflicts. When soldiers captured the Sioux who fought with Chippewa Chief Flat Mouth's band in 1827, they turned them over to the Chippewa for punishment by "running the gauntlet." This policy provoked the fiery Colonel Snelling to complain that the "military on this frontier are useless for want of discretionary power. . . . Men of Straw with wooden Guns will answer the same purpose." The army, however, interfered less and less in Indian matters as time went on, rarely imprisoning an Indian for some offense.

The man charged with responsibility for Indian affairs at Fort Snelling, however, was the Indian agent appointed and reappointed by four presidents of the United States from 1819 to 1839 — a colorful, opinionated, and incorruptible former army officer whose name was Lawrence Taliaferro (pronounced "Tol-i-ver"). Minnesota's pioneer historian, William W. Folwell, wrote that for twenty years Taliaferro was "the most important and the most influential civil servant on the upper Mississippi." Folwell recalled that Taliaferro "had two eminent qualifications for dealing with red men: one, absolute truthfulness; the other, a tolerance of Indian fondness for gaudy apparel, ceremonial, and oratory."

Although Pike had promised the Sioux in 1805 that the government would send an agent to serve them, fulfillment of that promise waited on the establishment

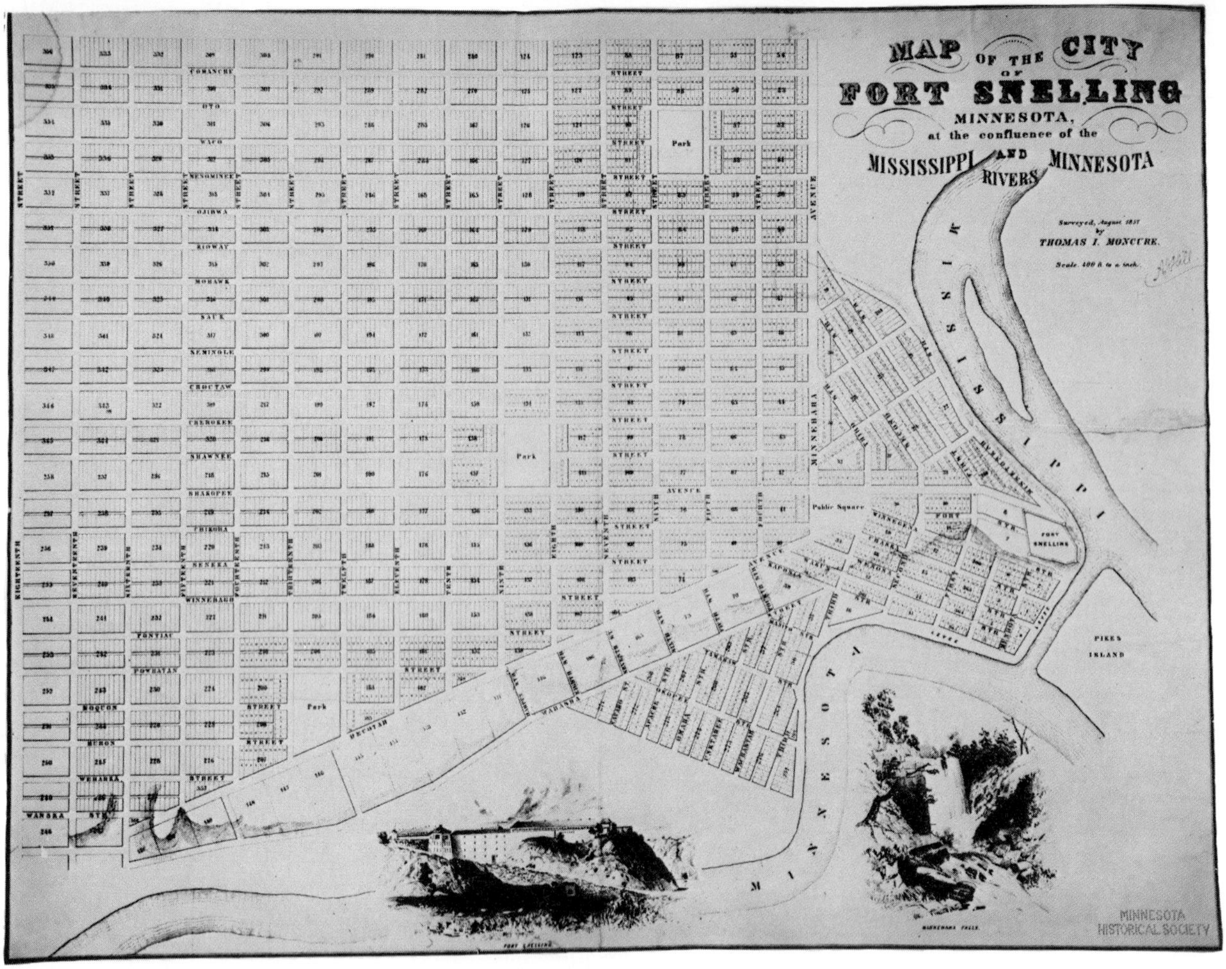

IN 1857 Fort Snelling was thought to have outlived its usefulness, and it was sold to Franklin Steele, a pioneer businessman who had once been a storekeeper at the post. He surveyed the land and planned the "City of Fort Snelling" shown above. Before the project made much progress, however, the Civil War erupted, and the old fort was reactivated as a rendezvous point for Minnesota volunteer troops.

> "Fort Snelling, with its 6,000 acres of reserve, was sold by Secretary Floyd to a Mr. Steele, who has paid $30,000, but failed to pay the balance. . . . The government took possession of the reservation at the breaking out of the war, and during the rebellion used it as a depot for collecting volunteer troops. The fort should be retained, and a compromise made with Mr. Steele."
> GENERAL WILLIAM T. SHERMAN,
> March 10, 1868

BEGINNING in the Civil War period, the fort began to expand beyond the old walls. The National Archives photograph below, taken about 1863, shows some of the frame buildings thrown up in those years. The two views above from that era are the only known photographic record of the gatehouse.

of a protective military post. Taliaferro, appointed by his fellow Virginian and friend, President James Monroe, made his way up the Mississippi on Leavenworth's heels, and, with the help of soldiers, set about the construction of several agency buildings about a quarter mile west of Fort Snelling.

The agent informed his curious Indian visitors that the president of the United States not the king of England was their Great Father. He welcomed the Indians at the agency day and night, and they regularly gathered in the friendly council house for talk and business. Taliaferro's success at exorcising latent British sympathies is indicated by the 36 medals of George III, 28 British flags, and 18 gorgets which were surrendered to him by various chiefs during his first two years.

To Taliaferro also fell the difficult role of personal mediator between the white and Indian civilizations. He was responsible for licensing all fur traders permitted in the Indian country, and for trying to arrange fair treaties to open the first Minnesota lands to white settlement. The former became an extremely trying task for Taliaferro whose uncompromising integrity and self-righteousness attracted the criticism and chicanery of men who resented his control over their profits. Only the existence of the fort's garrison lent weight to Taliaferro's decisions.

Across the river from the Indian agency and the fort — as if to challenge these two arms of government authority — was one of the most prosperous trading headquarters in the Northwest, the American Fur Company's Mendota post. With the arrival in 1834 of Henry H. Sibley as chief fur company agent, Mendota began to figure positively in the Americanization of the area. Sibley built what he described as "a substantial and commodious stone dwelling . . . the first . . . private residence in all of Minnesota and Dakota," which served as a hospitable guesthouse for travelers during several decades. Its owner later became Minnesota's first territorial representative in Congress and the first governor of the state.

Although Sibley himself was reasonably honest and fair in his dealings with the Indians, his fellow traders

THE PHOTOGRAPH above, taken in 1863, provided accurate details for the restoration of several buildings. The Round Tower (p) stands among wooden structures erected during the Civil War. The barracks (d) were originally used as a hospital. Between the barracks and the schoolhouse (g) is the only known photograph of the guardhouse (m). By studying it, researchers worked out the roof angle and the sizes of the windows. Courtesy National Archives.

CAREFUL ANALYSIS of the enlargement of the schoolhouse (1863) at left told researchers about the window and door placement, the slope of the roof, and suggested that a fireplace chimney had been replaced when stoves were installed to heat the structure. In the reconstructed building a second door was substituted for the right window as a temporary convenience to visitors. Courtesy National Archives.

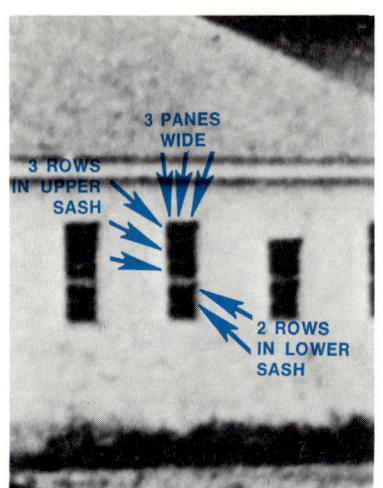

AN EXTREME ENLARGEMENT of the schoolhouse window from the photograph above revealed the pattern of the panes and indicated that sliding sashes were used. From lists of materials shipped to the post, researchers learned the size of the individual panes. The mullions (thin bars between the panes) were rebuilt in a style common in New England, since it was known that some of the carpenters among Snelling's troops enlisted there. The putty holding the glass in place was made from white lead and linseed oil shipped to the fort.

ARCHAEOLOGISTS located the foundations of the schoolhouse and the base of the suspected fireplace. The structure was reconstructed on the same site to the exact size of that built by Snelling's men.

HAND-BLOWN GLASS like that used in the 1820s was made for the reconstruction by a firm that makes stained glass for church windows. Notice the waves and bubbles, which are characteristic of glass made by this older method.

of the American Fur Company often disregarded government policies issued from Fort Snelling. A particularly thorny question, entangling the area's three centers of authority — the fort, the Indian agency, and the Mendota trading post — was the use of liquor. The "solution" to this problem is an interesting chapter in Minnesota history, significant to the growth of the state's urban centers.

Liquor in the form of cheap whisky or watered rum commanded an inflated value in the fur trade, but frequent incidents of drunkenness and disorder leading to serious crimes prompted Congress to legislate more or less unsuccessfully in 1832 that "no ardent spirits shall be hereafter introduced into Indian country."

Despite government policy, liquor was as highly regarded by the frontier troops as it was by the traders. It soon became apparent to military officials that soldiers who spent their days keeping whisky from the Indians spent their nights obtaining quantities for themselves from grogshops operated by squatters living near the fort. On one particularly debauched evening in 1839, 47 soldiers were confined for drunkenness, although it was well known that the offense was punishable by solitary confinement in the "Black Hole," as the guardhouse was called. Friction over the sale of liquor and other problems intensified until Commandant Joseph Plympton cleared settlers and liquor dealers alike from the military reservation. The last of the squatters' cabins was razed by the soldiers in 1840.

The civilian population around Fort Snelling during this period (approximately 150 of whom were white) included traders, half-breeds, Swiss refugees from the disaster-ridden Red River Colony, retired soldiers, and a few slaves. One of the latter was Dred Scott, whose residence at the post from 1836 to 1838 figured in the famous 1856 Supreme Court decision which heightened the national controversy over Negro slavery.

Valuing the protection of the fort, the squatters removed by Plympton settled immediately outside the reservation. Rude homes were thrown up downstream near the claim of Pierre "Pig's Eye" Parrant, a notorious, one-eyed whiskyseller. The settlement was at first known as "Pig's Eye" until more sensitive residents renamed it "St. Paul's," for the log chapel dedicated to

ONE OF THE FOUR remaining structures erected by Snelling is the commandant's house. Greatly altered over the years, it is shown above as it looked in 1861 when officers of the First Minnesota Volunteer Infantry posed before leaving for the Civil War. Notice the portico, the window details, and the stonework. Photograph by B. F. Upton.

A COMPARISON of the above drawing from McClure's 1835 plan with the photograph on the opposite page made it clear that the portico had been added to the commandant's house sometime between 1835 and 1861.

THE PHOTOGRAPH below shows the commandant's house as it looked in 1970. Although a second story was added and many other changes were made in 1904, elements of the original house remain to guide the restorers.

the apostle Paul in 1841. Eight years later St. Paul became the capital of Minnesota Territory. A few refugees settled at Mendota. Others squatted on land east of the Falls of St. Anthony near the government mills in an area that later became Minneapolis — the state's largest city.

As civilians voluntarily or involuntarily dissociated from the fort, they began to appreciate the great nonmilitary potential of the area. Treaties signed by the Chippewa and Sioux in 1837 officially opened the valuable lands between the St. Croix and Mississippi rivers to settlement. In the 1840s, pioneers like Henry M. Rice and Joseph R. Brown, as well as Eastern capitalists, began investing in primary industries such as lumbering and milling. Skeptics like Henry H. Sibley reconsidered their predictions that the Upper Mississippi Valley would never be more than sparsely populated.

A growing number of visitors as well as settlers came to the junction of the two rivers. Traders, missionaries, and explorers paused at Fort Snelling to gather supplies and information about the wilderness. George Catlin and other artists came to paint the Indians and the majestic scenery. Romantic pilgrims such as Count Giacomo C. Beltrami, a colorful Italian, and Mrs. Alexander Hamilton, widow of the famous statesman, rhapsodized over the post, likening it to a German castle on the Rhine. As steamboat service grew more regular, Fort Snelling became the high spot of the "Fashionable Tour" taken by the wealthy and the curious. In 1854 about a thousand excursionists were attracted to the fort and its environs, making tourism one of Minnesota's first major industries.

In the late 1840s and 1850s two events associated with the receding frontier permanently changed the function and character of Fort Snelling: the organization of the Minnesota Territory and the construction of new western forts. With the appointment of a territorial governor and other officials in 1849, many of Fort Snelling's earlier duties were assumed by the civilian government at St. Paul. Soldiers at the fort acted as a kind of "National Guard" to be called upon only when civilians were unable to handle a problem, although the post's guardhouse continued to serve as the only jail in the territory for some years.

**THE ROUND TOWER** is shown (left above) as it looked in its early years. The photograph, taken about 1861, confirmed other sources which indicated that it originally had no battlements. By 1863 (center) a conical roof covered the structure, which was then used for munitions storage. Badly gutted by fire in 1869, the old bastion was rebuilt (right) with battlements and windows added — factors which greatly complicated its restoration in the 1960s to the condition shown at left above. Over the years it served successively as a prison, offices, quarters, beauty shop, and in the 1930s and 1940s as a museum.

**A FOCAL POINT** of civic pride, the Round Tower became the best known of the four buildings remaining from the original fort by the late 19th and early 20th centuries. Under the auspices of the Daughters of the American Revolution, wreaths were laid at the tower in September, 1915, to mark the 91st anniversary of the laying of the cornerstone.

> *"Even as the history of the state of Minnesota is inextricably interwoven with the events that took place at old Fort Snelling . . . so is the familiar silhouette of the Round Tower a sturdy anchor for the fort itself. Standing like the prow of a ship at the prairie end of the diamond-shaped fort, the limestone tower pointed the way ever northwestward for the expanding American nation. Although there may be some question as to whether the Round Tower actually is the oldest building in the state, it is, beyond dispute, the most venerated symbol of Minnesota's early history."*
>
> JOHN M. CALLENDER, archaeologist, 1959

TO PRESERVE IT, the crumbling Round Tower (below left) was covered with stucco in 1904, but public outrage over the defacement forced its immediate removal. Reuben Warner, Jr. and friends (below right) drove out to inspect the progress of the removal later that year. Courtesy Minneapolis Public Library and H. E. Vanderwater.

As advancing white settlement surged beyond Fort Snelling, the old bastion's role as guardian of the northwestern border was taken over by Fort Ripley on the Mississippi River near Little Falls (1849) and Fort Ridgely on the Minnesota River near New Ulm (1853). Pressure for the opening of more land resulted in the signing of two treaties with the Sioux in 1851, which made available much of southern Minnesota to settlement and crowded the Indians farther up the Minnesota River.

No longer on the cutting edge of the westward-moving frontier, Fort Snelling became a supply depot for the new posts. Fort Crawford at Prairie du Chien was closed, and its troops were shifted to Snelling. There they lived in the stone barracks and officers' quarters which by 1847 had replaced the wooden buildings erected under Snelling's direction. Some were quartered in the old hospital which served as a barracks after 1840, when a larger hospital was created by adding a second story to the former shops building.

Fort Snelling's military significance declined sharply in the 1850s. In fact, the immediate area had become so settled and tranquil that C. K. Smith, the first secretary of Minnesota Territory, suggested in 1849 that the fort be turned into a branch of West Point so that it might serve the West as a military academy. As St. Paul grew in importance, the old post's principal function seemed for a time to be the providing of music for social gatherings. Its fine band enlivened life in early St. Paul by giving benefit concerts and playing for dances during a period when musicians were rare among the newly arrived settlers.

In 1857 Fort Snelling was suddenly sold to Franklin Steele, a pioneer businessman who had once served as sutler at the post. With the help of Henry M. Rice, Minnesota Territory's representative in Congress, Steele secured a seemingly obscure amendment to an act of 1819 reauthorizing the secretary of war to sell military sites "which are or may become useless for military purposes." Steele then asked Rice to write the secretary of war proposing that the government sell him Fort

BLACK TROOPS posed near the Hexagonal Tower about 1887. The road built by Snelling's troops once led down to the steamboat landing on the river. The same roadbed now serves the state park. Courtesy National Archives.

"In this old Fort we have one of the most interesting places in the frontier history of the country. . . . Every year these things become more valuable and interesting. . . . the old Fort, restored to its former state, would give us a place, unique in its character. There would be nothing like it in the United States. . . . If it is to be preserved it must pass under the control of some civil Society, for in the War Department there is neither romance nor sentiment."

GENERAL EDWIN C. MASON, commandant, 1895

OF THE FOUR original structures remaining when restoration began in 1965, the Hexagonal Tower had suffered the least alteration. It is shown (left above) as it looked when restoration began, and (right) after restoration had been completed.

ARMY MULES pulled a load of ice cut from the nearby river in the 1890s. The Hexagonal Tower and the deteriorating walls and commissary of the fort may be seen in the background.

Snelling. The secretary agreed, and, in a clandestine transaction, Steele purchased the entire military reservation (including a large part of present-day St. Paul and Minneapolis) for $90,000. Nine months later a House committee investigating the scandal stated that the sale had been made without legal authority and under noncompetitive conditions. But a hastily formed military committee maintained that the site *was* no longer useful, and the investigation was dropped.

On June 1, 1858, the troops marched out of the walled post which had served as a vanguard of settlement for 38 years. For some time thereafter visitors could watch sheep grazing on the once active paradeground or anticipate which lot they might purchase in Steele's proposed "City of Fort Snelling."

But events in other parts of the nation it had served so well decreed that the old post's retirement from active duty was to be brief. In April, 1861, the country found itself engaged in the Civil War. Because of its location near the centers of settlement and its well-constructed facilities, Fort Snelling was the logical place for Minnesota volunteers to rendezvous. Derelict in his payments, Steele agreed to Governor Alexander Ramsey's request that the post be reactivated, and Fort Snelling became the induction and training center for the First Minnesota (the first troops to volunteer for the Union Army) and for the other ten Minnesota infantry regiments which served in the Civil War.

Its new duties made necessary the renovation and enlargement of a garrison which had never housed so many men. Undermanned during all its years as a frontier sentinel, Fort Snelling had usually boasted a complement of less than 300 soldiers. Now it had to deal with as many as 2,000. Wooden barracks, storehouses, stables, and other minor buildings were constructed inside and outside the walls of the old fort, which grew physically to five times its original size.

Sixteen months after the first troops marched off to Civil War battlefields, the Minnesota countryside was convulsed in its own war. Dissident Sioux Indians — displeased with the location and quality of their reservation, provoked by winter starvation, and generally desperate about their future — attacked the Lower

THIS HEADQUARTERS building for the Department of Dakota was built on Taylor Avenue in the 1880s.

> "Recently a portion of its outer wall has fallen, caused by excavations for the track of a railroad, and, under the advancing and resistless pressure of modern civilization, it may be, that within a generation, not one stone will be left on another."
>
> EDWARD D. NEILL, historian, 1864

CRUMBLING WALLS and other evidences of deterioration may be seen in the photograph below, which was probably taken in the 1870s. As new structures were built to serve changing military needs, the old walled fort became less and less useful. Photograph by W. H. Illingworth from a wet plate negative.

FORT SNELLING, MINNESOTA, ON THE CHICAGO, MILWAUKEE AND ST. PAUL R. R.

THE CHANGES which began during the Civil War continued throughout the 19th century as the role of Fort Snelling shifted from frontier outpost to headquarters and supply depot for the Department of Dakota. When this engraving was published in the *Independent Farmer and Fireside Companion* in 1879, the forerunner of today's Milwaukee Railroad had laid tracks along the Mississippi River below the fort's walls, and the semicircular lookout battery had been roofed to serve as a summer porch.

Sioux Indian Agency on the Minnesota River in August, 1862. Led by Chief Little Crow, they quickly spread death and terror throughout the Minnesota Valley. Fort Ridgely and New Ulm were attacked (unsuccessfully) before Henry H. Sibley was hastily commissioned by the governor to pursue and punish the rebellious Indians. Commanding an untrained body of volunteers and the officerless remnant of the Third Minnesota Regiment which had been paroled from a Southern prison, Sibley defeated a large Sioux force in the battle of Wood Lake on September 23, 1862. With that, organized Indian resistance in Minnesota came to an end.

Many implicated Sioux escaped to Dakota Territory. Another 1,700 Indians who had surrendered to Sibley's troops were corralled on the Minnesota River flats below Fort Snelling, where they spent a disastrous winter. Later the survivors were removed to Dakota Territory. There some Sioux continued to fight the white man and to reject reservation life throughout the 1870s and 1880s.

Soon after peace was made with the Minnesota Sioux and the South, the war department decided to keep Fort Snelling as a permanent army post — possibly at the suggestion of the distinguished Civil War general, William T. Sherman, who visited the garrison in 1866. In 1871 Fort Snelling was formally transferred from Steele back to the government. It served primarily as a supply depot for the many outposts which were established on the Great Plains in the 1860s and 1870s.

During the 1880s the federal government adopted a new policy of maintaining fewer and larger army posts in the West. Accordingly, Fort Snelling was selected in 1881 as administrative headquarters for the Department of Dakota — a system of some 18 frontier forts which supervised Indian and civilian affairs throughout Dakota and Montana territories. Fort Snelling also served as the principal arms and provisions depot for these posts. Only rarely were its troops called into the field. Occasionally, however, the garrison took up its old duties of subduing the Indians. In 1881 its help was required at the Indian agency near Green Bay, Wisconsin, and in 1898 soldiers were dispatched to Leech Lake, where their presence quickly quelled a rebellion among the Chippewa Indians.

ONE of many frame structures erected near Taylor Avenue in the last half of the 19th century was the scene of the funeral of six soldiers killed in the uprising of Leech Lake Chippewa in 1898. Note the horse-drawn Victorian hearses.

TROOPS of the Third Infantry boarded streetcars on January 30, 1898, for the first leg of their journey to Manila and service in the Spanish-American War. The presence of streetcar tracks and roads were among the many factors that complicated archaeological investigations of the fort site in the 1950s and 1960s.

ARTILLERY PRACTICE is shown in 1918, when the fort served as a training center during World War I. It performed a similar function in World War II.

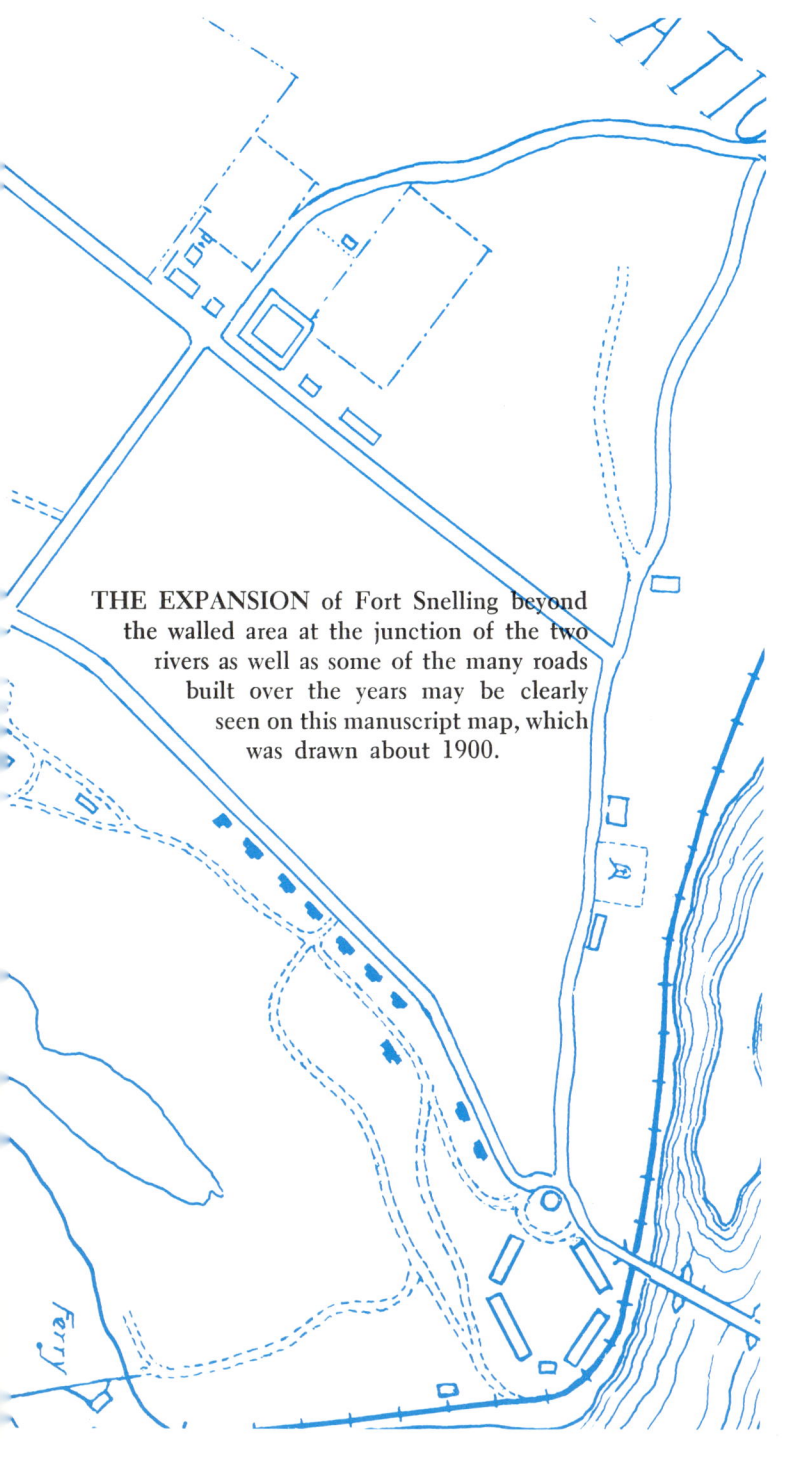

THE EXPANSION of Fort Snelling beyond the walled area at the junction of the two rivers as well as some of the many roads built over the years may be clearly seen on this manuscript map, which was drawn about 1900.

While the fort acquired additional officers' quarters and barracks outside the old walls to accommodate the larger number of troops stationed there, the older buildings were allowed to deteriorate. In 1869 a fire gutted the interior of the Round Tower. In 1885 a quartermaster general summarized the conditions of various buildings as "crowded," "unfit for habitation," "a fire trap," and "a ruin." Sections of the walls crumbled throughout the 1870s and 1880s; the schoolhouse, Pentagonal Tower, and the lookout were dismantled.

The fort's disrepair did not pass entirely unnoticed. Many individuals felt that a site which had played such an important role should be preserved. General E. C. Mason, commandant in 1895, articulated this concern when he spoke at a celebration to commemorate the 75th anniversary of the laying of the cornerstone. With considerable foresight, Mason proposed a limited restoration and the conversion of the buildings into a museum, but his suggestion was virtually ignored for over half a century.

Concerned with efficiency rather than history, the war department in 1901 ordered that the officers' quarters be torn down. Considerable damage was done before a citizens' committee persuaded the post commander to intercede. Two years later, the commander obtained approval of his own plan for remodeling the fort. Minnesotans, uneasy about rumors that it was being "restored" beyond recognition, were assured by the *St. Paul Pioneer Press* of July 19, 1903, that the Round Tower was only to be "strengthened" and the parapets replaced "to make it look as it did in days gone by." The following year the tower was covered with unsightly white stucco, but such an outcry arose that it was soon chipped off. In 1904, however, second stories were added to the commandant's house and the officers' quarters, which were remodeled on a Spanish theme obscuring the primitive flavor of the buildings.

Over the years while Fort Snelling was serving as a training center for officers and an induction-discharge station for Minnesota troops in World Wars I and II, "progress" waged its own war. The old bridge to St. Paul (built in 1880) was replaced by a larger one in

A CONTROVERSIAL PLAN for a new freeway proposed in 1956 proved to be the catalyst for restoration and reconstruction of the fort. Public protest led to the building of a highway tunnel to preserve the fort site and the four remaining buildings.

In 1961 the Minnesota legislature established Fort Snelling State Historical Park, and four years later appropriated the first funds to begin reconstruction of the historic old fort.

ARCHAEOLOGISTS then began a careful and thorough excavation of the old building sites, thoroughly screening each shovel of dirt for buttons, bottles, and other evidences of life at the post.

DURING the first year of work, masons laid stone for the guardhouse, duplicating as nearly as possible the methods used by Snelling's troops in the 1820s. The Round Tower, with its battlements, may be seen in the background as it looked when restoration began.

RESEARCH indicated that wooden pickets had once existed atop a portion of the wall. They may be seen at left in this photograph of the restored wall and guardhouse. This boarded section of the wall was the only portion walked by the guards.

THE ROUND TOWER, well, powder magazine, and sutler's store are shown here in the last stages of restoration and reconstruction. Note that the battlements have been removed from the tower, and the central column supports a flagpole.

1909, and in 1926 the Mendota Bridge was constructed, creating a complex system of roads near and through the fort grounds. To ease public concern a small museum was set up in the Round Tower in the 1930s and maintained for six years with the aid of Works Progress Administration funds. In 1946, however, the war department announced that Fort Snelling was being permanently retired as an army post. On October 14, 1946, the flag was lowered for the last time, and Fort Snelling's 126 years of service as a military post came to an end. The museum was closed; the entire facility was turned over to the Veterans Administration.

During the next decade preservationists, who felt that the original features remaining of Snelling's fort (the Round and Hexagonal towers, the greatly altered commandant's house and officers' quarters, and the roadbed to the river) should be protected, tried to secure official recognition of the site. They failed in their attempts to have the area designated as a national monument or a state park, and not until 1960 were they successful in having the site recognized as a national historic landmark.

In the interval the Minnesota Highway Department in 1956 announced plans to construct a much-needed freeway *through* the old fort grounds — with a cloverleaf loop encircling the Round Tower. Barraged by public protest over this plan, Governor Orville L. Freeman mediated the dispute, ordering the construction of a 450-foot tunnel north of the fort through which traffic could flow with minimal disturbance to the historic setting.

Interest generated by the highway debate and the state centennial in 1958 prompted the Minnesota Statehood Centennial Commission to grant $25,000 to the Minnesota Historical Society for an archaeological exploration of the walled area of the old fort. Sixteen months of digging amid the water mains, sewer pipes, and telephone cables which crisscrossed the post grounds uncovered the foundations of nearly half of the original structures. This centennial excavation, reported Russell W. Fridley, director of the Minnesota Historical Society, "proved beyond question that a restoration of

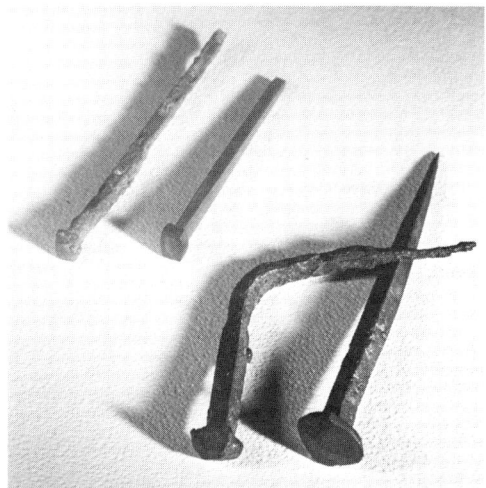

EVEN the nails for the restoration are replicas of those used in the 1820s. Cut nails (left), which were most common in the period, are still available for concrete work. Rosehead nails (right), which must bend to fasten hardware, were reproduced by the blacksmith.

HARDWARE for the restoration was made by a blacksmith, while he also demonstrated the craft to visitors.

IN THIS VIEW of the restoration, at left is the powder magazine (foreground), sutler's store, and unrestored officers' quarters (background). At right is the temporary blacksmith shed, the reconstructed wall with its wooden pickets, and the guardhouse, a portion of which served as a lime storage room.

Fort Snelling is not only possible but highly favored by the richness and extent of the remains of the post."

In 1961 several events brought the preservation and restoration of the site closer to realization. In his inaugural address Governor Elmer L. Andersen vigorously supported the establishment of a state park which included the old fort site. Recognizing that historical experiences as well as natural beauty are resources to be conserved, he urged the legislature to act on the "almost incredible" opportunity of creating a historical park in the heart of the Twin Cities urban area.

Responding to Governor Andersen's plea, the 1961 legislature established Fort Snelling State Historical Park — 2,500 wooded and watered acres, including the confluence of the two rivers, the site of Leavenworth's Cantonment New Hope, Pike Island, and, of course, the old limestone fort. An initial $65,000 was appropriated to begin acquiring privately owned portions of the tract.

Two years later the newly created Minnesota Outdoor Recreation Resources Commission investigated the feasibility of rebuilding Snelling's fort as an exciting focal center in the new recreational area. Upon the enthusiastic recommendation of the commission, a ten-year program for complete restoration and reconstruction was introduced and approved by the legislature in 1965. The estimated cost of $2 million was to be met by funds from federal and state governments and the contributions of private citizens.

A historian, an archaeologist, an architect, and a co-ordinator from the Minnesota Historical Society then began to assemble facts about the old fort. They read and compared early descriptions of the post, studied photographs and paintings (particularly those of the soldier-artist, Captain Seth Eastman), and dug for archaeological clues in order to duplicate exactly the buildings and furnishings used by Colonel Snelling and his men.

Actual reconstruction and restoration began in 1966, and by 1970 nearly half of the original structures were rebuilt. When the restoration is complete, a piece of the early 19th-century American Northwest will have been recreated in the heart of a 20th-century urban area, reminding visitors of a nearly forgotten, though not far removed, frontier heritage.

"It was for the 'Upper Country' that this fort was built—a country stretching from the Great Lakes across the wooded headwaters of the Mississippi and Minnesota rivers to the plains of the Missouri. . . . Fort Snelling became part of a comprehensive system for the protection of the frontier."

MARCUS L. HANSEN, historian, 1918